Wild Strawberries

Also By Eric Greinke

*Sand & Other Poems**
*Caged Angels**
10 Michigan Poets (as Editor)*
*The Last Ballet**
*Iron Rose**
Masterpiece Theater (with Brian Adam)*
*The Broken Lock (Selected Poems 1960-1975)**
Whole Self / Whole World - Quality of Life in the 21st
    *Century**
Sea Dog - A Coast Guard Memoir
Selected Poems 1972-2005
The Art of Natural Fishing
The Drunken Boat & Other Poems From The French Of
    Arthur Rimbaud

* *Out of Print*

Wild
Strawberries

poems by
Eric Greinke

PRESA :S: PRESS
Rockford, Michigan

Copyright © 2008 Eric Greinke

ACKNOWLEDGMENTS

These poems have appeared or are forthcoming in the following publications: *Backwards City Review, Barbaric Yawp, Bathtub Gin, Beatlick News, Big Scream, California Quarterly, Drama Garden, Free Verse, The Hurricane Review, Ibbetson St., The Iconoclast, Illogical Muse, Inside The Outside - An Anthology Of Avant-Garde American Poets, Magazine Six, Main Channel Voices, Muses Review, Napalm Health Spa Report, The New York Quarterly, The Pedestal, Presa, Small Press Review, Solo Café, Tar Wolf Review, Tertulia Magazine, The Unrorean, Wavelength, WestWard Quarterly, Wilderness House Literary Review, Wild Goose Poetry Review, & Words of Wisdom. Green Onions* first appeared as a broadside with Mark Sonnenfeld, Marymark Press, 2005. *The Run* first appeared as *Two Sonnets*, a limited edition broadside with Harry Smith, Presa Press, 2006. Some of the poems also appeared in the following chapbooks: *For The Living Dead*, Free Books, 2007 & *Up North* (with Harry Smith), Presa Press, 2006.

FIRST EDITION

PRINTED IN THE UNITED STATES OF AMERICA

ISBN: 978-0-9800081-1-1

Library of Congress Control Number: 2007938481

Cataloging Information: 1. Greinke, Eric, 1948 -
2. Contemporary American Poetry

PRESA :S: PRESS
PO Box 792   Rockford, Michigan 49341
presapress@aol.com   www.presapress.com

Contents

Wild Strawberries

Edges & Spaces

Lonely Planets

For The Living Dead

Life is an illusion.
Compassion fills my heart
For those who don't know the truth.
                    - Milarepa

Wild Strawberries

Heart Berries

Heart shaped
Wild strawberries
Redden on low strings
Their ineffable fragrance
Attracts the spirits
Of the dead
To stop & refresh themselves
On their journeys

Indians called them
Heart berries
They ate them
At the beginning of summer
To make them brave
For the rest of the year

In Another Time

I tell myself a dream to go
Into the yellow stone
That sings inside my throat.
The sky is grey & sweet.
My heart is an abandoned planet.

Even as I launch this tiny ship,
Someone looks for me
In the populated soil.
My ancestors roll in the waves.
Their vain blood floods my bed.

I tell myself today's old lines.
Today's old lines are mine.
Alone with you, myself.
Another birth, & other words.

In another time.

Leelanau Fire

The night is white.
The moon, a cosmic smile.
Big wind frightens a fawn.
A branch falls, an alarm.

For awhile, I remember
Pictures across the river,
A life boat in the snow,
Radio squawking at the stars.

Now images are gone.
Mind empty, I'm alone.
Right here, by the smoke
Of the glowing embers,

Camping on the edge
Of the open sky.

Dilemma

A broad-tailed hawk is using our winter bird-feeder for bait. Yesterday, we watched while it plucked grey feathers from a song sparrow & ate her. We grieved for the sparrow, feared for the chickadees & the two sets of cardinal mates.

You urged me to shoot it, but wouldn't we hate to see the hawk starve just as much? Frozen in ambivalence, I wait, not sure what I'll do if I see red down floating on a cold wind.

Black Flies

In the north woods, the black flies are as constant & insidious as time. They circle persistently at high speed around your head until your attention is distracted, then they dive in for a mouthful of your temporal flesh. Only wind & rain bring transitory relief from their eternal onslaught.

Nature Preserve

In the woods behind my home
Is a Nature Preserve
Its central feature is a lake
It takes me about an hour
To walk around it

There are no dogs allowed
No fires, no swimming, no
Boating, no metal detectors, no
Camping, no horses, no
Picnics, no   no

I am to fish only
In designated areas
I am to walk clockwise
Around the lake, or be
Stopped by the tall, steel turnstile

Last winter, the newspaper
Printed a letter from a group
of malcontents who crusaded
To get rid of the beavers
For chewing down the birch trees

Another group began a campaign
To get rid of the dread
Purple loosestrife, a tall flower
That grows by the waters edge
In a manner offensive to nature

Right now, the focus is on
The distasteful blue spruce
Which the officials of the preserve
Deem to be opportunistic
& unwelcome among the natives

They're building a trail
That will penetrate to the heart
Of the wildest part of the park
Leading from the Township Center
Easy access for all

Who prefer their wildlife preserved

Green Wood

I built my cabin
In the spring
Of my 37th year,
With freshly milled,
Bark-covered,
Inch-thick shimwood,
Mostly oak,
With some cherry mixed in.

A friend worked
For a lumber mill,
& got it for me for free.
The wood was swollen,
Heavy & green.
Sap bubbled
Around the spikes
As I drove them in.

I burned through
Two sabre-saws
Cutting through
The wet, green wood.
A year later,
When it cured,
It was so hard & dark
That no nail could penetrate.

Isolated Incident

Low grey clouds
Breathed a chill warning.
The smell of ice
Was in the air.
As darkness fell
I could hear
Whispers of flakes
Falling in the dark.

Next morning,
From where I stood
On the covered porch,
A series of footprints
Led off toward
The old logging road
That climbs the hill
Behind my hidden cabin.

Someone had stopped
While I slept.
Maybe a hunter
With a head start
On daybreak,
Or did the hunted
Take a break
From the snow

Before the last cold hill?

Stumps

Stumps of a proud generation
Tables of green moss
On a carpet of brown & yellow needles
Blue jay pounds a nut
Red squirrel chitters territory
A roof of tall white pines
Progeny of stumps

Whole counties of stumps
Villages of stumps
Houses of salamanders & centipedes
So much furniture
Left out in the rain
Wood aromatic in wet dew
Shrinking back from its own bark

Tractor In Field

The old tractor dreams in a field of snow. The tires are flat & cracked, fenders red with rust, elderly flywheel locked tight. It hasn't had a drink in years, though the rain washed over the rusty steel saddle where no one ever sits.

Old Boathouse

The old boathouse smells like heaven on spring mornings. The aroma of wet hemp ropes coiled on the deck mixes with the smell of the thawing earth on the bank & the fresh smell of the river, free of ice. The smell triggers a flurry of sweet visions & timeless associations.

A continuous gurgle of water over the rocks on the far side of the fast-moving river plays musical accompaniment to the aromatic high.

Sitting with eyes closed, I hesitate to add sight to this already delicious meal.

Chain Of Lakes

Now the lake
Has pulled her warmth
Down, to the bottom,
& swept her floors.

Bright green shoots
Of milfoil & cabbage
Line our shores
To form a green matte.

Pilots of small planes
See the deepest places.
The wind flakes the cold
Top water into whitecaps.

They channel on the breeze
That blows in from Quebec,
The brisk Northern wind
That pushes migratory geese

On a path of glacial footprints.

Ice Storm

10,000 white pines
Bowed to earth.
Grass became
Glass spikes.
Snow on the ground
Crusted over,
Hard enough
To support small animals.
Lightning glimmered
Across the yellow sky,
Reflected on the snow
By a loud roll
Of winter thunder.

Whitefish Point Light

The pebble beach
Is bleached to white,
Littered with ribcages of fish
& carcasses of big brown beetles.

More tankers & freighters
Sank off this point
Than anywhere in the Great Lakes.
The morning mist is thick

With sailors' ghosts.
Sometimes they appear as whitecaps
In broad daylight,
Trying to rise above the surf

That tore them from this life.

Bois Blanc Island

The beach is littered with rocks.
It was an underwater reef
Before the waters receded.
Now, an island of cedars & pines.

Bats rise in large numbers
From the tallest cedars.
They own the sky for an hour
Before & after nightfall.

Packs of coyotes chortle
As they break sticks past
My night window.
They are bold at dusk.

When their gray forms appear
On the rock-strewn beach,
It looks as if the rocks
Move inland, escaping rising water.

The Sun-Dance People

The Sun-Dance People seek dreams
When life is at a turning point

The Sun-Dance People don't mind
If a warrior stays home or leaves a battle

A large red bird flies through the room
You can't see it, but you feel it

You can hear the flapping of its huge wings
While little voices whisper in your ears

These are the Sun-Dance People

Paul Bunyan

Descended from Ice Giants of old, Paul Bunyan had an epic appetite. After he ate all the flapjacks in Northern Minnesota, he turned ominously toward Wisconsin's cheese & beer. Once he'd consumed those resources, which scientists had previously thought were boundless, Paul Bunyan was mighty thirsty, & that's the reason the water level in Lake Michigan went down another ten feet.

Sasquatch

Sasquatch wanders the Pacific Northwest, famous for the size of his feet. He shies away from contact with humans, despite his greater strength. He reeks.

We like to think that Sasquatch is a gentle vegetarian, but his stature implies a high need for animal protein, AKA *meat*.

A giant, carnivorous, reclusive mountain ape, Sasquatch is the boogieman of the coniferous forest. We search for him in vain, & speculate that he may be the missing link.

Sasquatch hides, & bides his time.

Beaver Territory

In spring the water
In Pickerel Lake
Is deep & clear
Blue like the sky

It overflows
To three smaller ponds
Cascading loudly
White water splashes over rocks

Now green summer
Is over
& the water
Is shallow

Matted by lily pads
Choked by
Rotting pickerel weed
Surrounding open water

Broken only
By beaver channels
Aquatic pathways
For mallards & swans

We pick our way
Around the lake
The path is blocked
By fallen birches

Razed
By the industry
Of the beavers
Tall birch trees

Taken down
Just for their branches
Whole groves fallen
With tooth marks

On the few
That still stand
We think it must be
The work of several beavers

So we get up early
To observe them
At their work
But they retreat to the lake

To warn us away with slapping tails

Northern Lights

A roar of jeweled leaves
Titillates the dark northern sky
Celebration above the trees
Aurora flares
Sun spots dance the edge
Owl turns to small sound
Marten clings
To a red pine branch
Outside my sleepy head

Liquid

Wild ducks
Scoot a landing
On blue eyes

Kayak Lesson

Balance is everything in a kayak. In the wind, you must paddle harder on one side, just to go straight. Keep your nose pointed at the bow. Keep the bow pointed at your destination. Keep your back straight. Momentum will continue after you stop paddling, but the wind may turn you in a circle. You will have to get straight by digging deep, making every stroke count. In gentle water, little strokes yield big distances. In rough water, timing is the key to keeping your balance. If you lean one way, just a little, the kayak will go the opposite way. If you stop paddling, balance becomes more difficult. Better to find a rhythm that you can maintain. Direction, concentration, perception. You become the paddle, the kayak, the ocean itself.

Fast Water

for Mark Workman

When you launch your kayak into a fast-running river, you don't have time to warm-up or practice. The power of the river catches you, & plummets you forward like relentless time.

Rocks loom in your path. You must react immediately, or you'll crash into them. Big rocks are easy to see, but submerged rocks must be identified by standing-wave, backsplash or dimple. You must read the river.

A rippled area may signify a flat rock, barely below the surface. You can surf-up on a flat rock & get stuck there. Then, the river can spin you around like a clock.

Sometimes the river spins you halfway around, then releases you, to continue downriver, backward. Then, you look at where you've been, back in time.

Going backward is dangerous, because you can't see the obstacles as you careen inevitably onward.

Back Home

Winter is here.
The air is chilly & crisp.
Field mice have moved inside.
Many thoughts crowd my mind
& grief clouds my heart.
Many songs press for words,
But who will sing them?
The morning wind invades my shirt.
The light of the moon dissipates,
& the sirens moan
As I fly myself back home.

Swiss Army

My favorite tool
Is not too heavy,
Not too light.

It's served me food,
Fished out lost knots,
Revealed the intricacies

Of nature, under
Its magnifying
Glass, & more.

Sometimes,
It was my only knife.
From Cape May to

Keweenaw Bay,
I reached for it
Often,

Grateful
For all my trusty
Attachments.

Wild Strawberries

Coming across them
Unexpectedly, as
A child, they
Taste as fresh
As red. Hard
To collect enough
To bring home
For jam, so we
Eat them while we can.

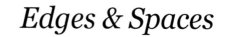

Edges & Spaces

Dust

Obnoxious cosmetics
Drip from the face
Of the Statue of Liberty.

Diamonds gleam
From the President's teeth.

Old dogs argue
Over the skulls
Of rock stars & senators.

A battalion of metal roaches
Dances around a captured flag.

In the middle
Of the moonless night
Old men remember the Third Reich.

Alarms ring in gladiolas,
Cueballing yet another Spring.

Search & Rescue

1.
Supersonic horseshoes whiz
Past barbecued executives

Molten doughboys push their buns
Through networks of static tranquilizers

Whole blood on special sale
Blue bunnies have found the eggs

A hawk sails symbolically, hunting
Friendly chickadees, happy in morning sunlight

Loud, obvious spaces blurt out
Streams of angry money, accusing

2.
Grey morning clouds over the straits
Blue noise lights the sky

Old men follow without desire
Wildfires race each day to play

Sweet pine fragrance, crisp A.M. air
A loud chunk of chocolate breaks off

Shrill politicians whittle down the branches
Deer bed down for the day, afraid

Many of the hardest games
Were never played, until that day

3.
In the candy penitentiary
In the bloody popcorn theater

After the backward horse race
Often, but not always, predictable

On a distant planet, light years away
On top of Old Smoky, coughing

When all the trees are dormant
Barricades no one can pass

All masks removed at last
Big pike glide between lilies, predatory

Desire

1: SKIN CANALS
Snakes fly toward the sun
Elements form a grammar

Spherical bodies rotate in space
Hollow noise of surf is heard

A game of hide & seek began
Round stones rose from sand

A stranger ran, hammer in hand
Against the mountains of the sun

A connection between snakes & men
A legend in the tiny islands

2: AFTER THE ROBBERY
Searchers return, bereft
Armed in suits of platinum

Even if the coffins were illusions
War broke out among the ruins

A crocodile lost its way
East or west to a fixed position

The stranger came again to play
Available in this space age

Refugees, constricted, extricate
In inexplicable picturesque epics

3: MAD MOUNTAINS
Solid stone broke the diamond saw
An iridescent surface had been formed

Departure gyrated a gentle beat
Teenagers brought the fresh roots

Without warning, there's the ruins
You find no steps, nor stairs

Consorted shapes were formed
Four balls dangled like musical notes

Gas sends out a beam of light
Sure to appear as simple ornamentation

The Light

1.
In a strange, low voice
In the middle of the winter

It is mandatory to deceive
It makes us want to leave

Like an old hammer on the bench
Like people drunk in a dream

My shoes are covered with dust
My tactics are confusing

Someone is always leaving
Someone else covers up the crimes

2.
The rain is the key
The dolls are asleep

There are books in the field
There are boxes of pain

This is where I see it
This light, this sleep, this touch

This is where you dropped it
This memory, this vision of wind

We must make plans
We see the victims, hear their songs

3.
Someone arrived late for
Someone else, who died

Someone came in, afraid that
Someone horrible hid outside

Like a box of raisins, spilled
Like pebbles on the beach

My imaginary range astonishes
My imaginary audience

You dropped the book, picked up the key
You put the dolls to sleep, put out the light

Spaces

1. THE VOID
Ornamental bones
Climb ladders of disaster

A hot breeze laughs
Always wild & welcome

Perpetual pinpricks
Maintain their eternal courses

Shadows vanish in the night
Nothing in the mirror but light

I walk toward ruin
Guided only by the moon

2. OLD PENNIES
Many men remain mad
At Descartes, who split

Kierkegaard took a flying leap
Camus sank a camouflaged canoe

Nietzsche growled into the mirror
Jean Paul Sartre played it smart

Tzara took off his tiara
Blake jumped in the lake

Army surplus tanks
Shoot blanks into the banks

3. WILDERNESS HOTEL

A loud act of love
Shakes the foundation

Falling trees scream freely
Abandoned avenues echo no more

An egg, emotionally crushed
No one gets the joke

A van vanishes down a long road
A sound drowns in silence

We reserve our opinions
Our private parking spaces

Masks

1.
Clouds of joy rain painfully
On toy villages, temporarily ephemeral

Feeble trees emit intermittent screams
Samples of noise impregnate imperviously

A mouthful of antique coins
An earful of 3rd degree love

Shoreline tents, leopard skinned
Starlight on pink steel bridges

Inspirational bloodbuckets
Strain the concerts, emphatic

2.
Cockroaches, successful in longevity
Raise the standard of experience

Neurotic beasts cry bitterly
On beaches of plastic popcorn

Boxes of big dreams are filed
In hope chests & sour trunks

A surrender is signed
In 4/4 time, appalling

Alternative habits, none feasible
Mask a blatant truth, shameful

3.
Blue heron stalks, motionless
Spear marks appear anonymously

Another ridiculous brainstorm
More mirth, defective but elastic

A strategic withdrawal, brave friend
Neglected correspondence, indignant

But wisely alone, inventive
Powerful, mercilessly noble

Dealers imagine victories
Over those who starve, gold-toothed

Hard Edges

1: SMOG
Bloody soldiers lie like sticks
On a hurricane beach

Bionic limbs replace shot off
Branches, grotesque woodpiles

A posse of insane clowns tunes up
Guided by the grinding wheels of half-tracks

Shells scream through the morning mist
Black smoke swirls over abandoned boots

We're still marching in perfect order
Into the red-stained, funeral smog

2: HIGH NOON
Petty criminals take a hard line
Defending the borders of their minds

A militia of monkeys reigns
Over the temporarily insane drains

Laughter breaks the structure
Of mirages we run over

The sun implores us to behave
But the moon plays ever after

Even on the best of days
The story gets shorter

3: ROCK GARDEN
Dungeons in the skull
Of an abstract elephant

A storm at sea
Through time & space

Such as Stonehenge
Labyrinths of bone, so old

Working from ropes, walkways,
Airships, cranes & towers

More than 15 million species
Rolling & forming, texturing & firing

Transmigration

1.
A torch of morning birds flares
Joyful bubbles of music explode

Redundant black bear on the back deck
Disoriented curiosity of the wild

Dark wounds on drunken willows
Celebrate knots of green light

Hearts glow from old houses
Where candles burned like dreams

Linking flesh beyond limits
We scratch across intentional walls

2.
In rooms down the hall
Priests wield ritual implements

Lay folk kneel in awe
Rain returns as we leave the lodge

Lingering by the plexiglass partition
Like a yellow blanket on a river bed

You slouch in the back row
Staring blindly out the window

Quick locks broke keys up
Imagined as overgrown paths

3.
The dead whisper insistently
The October wind gives in

In the blood-filled eye
Of the next hurricane

In a year of death by drowning
& honor gained by refusing honor

Emptied of pressing desire
Eternally firing but lethal

The letters labored under parched parchment
Sure sign of a moral compass

Green Onions

Fresh verve
From Booker T.
Reminds me
Of my great grandfather,
Jazzing it up
Among the carrots
& green onions.

I drive through
The ghetto
Flinging handfuls
Of brave pennies.
I deny
Any symbolic intent,
Crisp & hot on my tongue.

Lonely Planets

Lonely Planets

Exploding supernovae
Spread particles
Across the galaxy.
We still live
In that ocean, we
Carry it around
In our cells.

Ice fishing on Europa,
We wonder
What might lurk
Beneath the surface.
Our eyes are the water
In the ocean of stars.
We can taste it in our tears.

Go Fish

for George Cooley

1.
Maximum heads
Roam ceaselessly
Across the globe
Lone rangers in cyberspace

An infinite variety
Of sentient creatures
Their lights
Turned off, then on

Green spring buds
In wind off lake
Sleeping in the wind
Better than a swim

I am every kind
Of fool, yet cool
As a kingfisher
Staring into blue

2.
Mysterious glades
Shelter frightened fanatics
Binderies of fun
Collate the bad news

A humanitarian legacy
Three bolognas
Rotten teeth, bad breath
Bad black holes

Political agendas
Stink up the galaxy
Stalked in stockings
Born to run away

Lost civilizations
In the tired sky
I blink, drink water
Fish disappear

Initial Contact

An avalanche
Of confused emotion
Suffocates some
Surprised skiers.

Space above,
Fathoms below,
Blind, florescent cave fish
Are oblivious to pressure,
Or tidal waves.

The science of silence,
A mystery, rewinds.
Okay, but what's that shadow
Passing inexorably
Over the fragile mountains?

What is that sky? What
Have you done
To my moon, mother?
Why does it seem
To snow forever?

In Space

You need your space.
You need to screen
Your calls.
You must be careful
With opinion polls.

The faster you go
The more energy
It takes. You have
A pattern of memories
That confirm your beliefs.

You have seen
The little creatures.
You have sent
Symbolic broadcasts,
Sitcoms, talk-shows, commercials.

"But what about the spaceships?"
You ask, remembering a time.

Isla Morte

Fallen leaves bury
Surrounding memory
Flooded
Shoreline endures
Gentle passage
Yellow roses burn
Frail chickadees
In shadows of trees
Shiver in their sleep
Space to breathe
Other lights
Answer
Human faces
Naked outcasts

Perspective

I wish I was
An astronaut.
I could gesture
Magnanimously
At the whole world
From 1000 miles
Away, & never worry

With all the universe
Behind me,
& only the blue sphere
Of planet earth
Floating before me
I'd never worry
That we might drift apart

Summer Storm

Flying leaves & branches
Smacked the window panes
With violent thuds & bangs
Within the desperate sound
Of still-rising wind
Thick with blasting sand

The curtains were drawn
Thick & warm
While the tantrum rain
Flooded the muddy garden
& the roses, in pain
Made their final stand
Against the giant hand

Garment

Light emanates from my coat
My coat that contains
A shining stream
My coat of fool's gold
Wiser than the stars
Singing in its pockets
Imprisoned by the fragrance
Of the rosy clouds
Like the dark heart
Hidden in a bright cave
Hidden in infinity
So far out in the open
That little fish
Swim through its fabric

Old Woman's Dream #2

I slept in a house made of flesh. The floors were soft & spongy, & had the colors & textures of skin, from a rich black to a glowing pink. I walked on them barefoot, & could feel the warmth of the house, its breath & the beating of its heart. The house smelled like spearmint. It had a big window on each wall. One looked out on a desert; one revealed a northern forest; the third eye saw underwater, & there were many pretty tropical fish. When I looked out the last window, I saw into a living room just like the one I had become a part of.

Sterling

Tall shafts of air
On the frigid edge
Watery light sparkles
Hits the choppy rapids
Leaves an avocado tint
Splashes against the banks
Freely confused
A stained glass sunrise
In frosty shadows
Reckless silver tarpon
Flies to blue sunlight
Becoming small
A wave breaks
Over an icy wall

Bad Signs

There were gaping holes
In the roof.
The rotted floorboards
Were scattered
With broken glass,
Rusted screws & bolts,
& pieces of flattened iron
That used to be
Part of something larger,
A long time ago.

A big black mongrel
Guarded an old couch,
& chewed on a pair
Of stained girl's cutoffs.

A chain-link fence
Ran for a mile
Along the dusty road,
Posted with
Bright orange
HAZARD signs,
& bright yellow
NO TRESPASSING signs,
All of them
Riddled with bullet holes.

The Terms

Mute witness to these killings
Doors slam forever
In your famous nightmares
Blood stains forever
The Swiss Army reputation
When you take the gloves off
You find they still fit

For a moment
The Emperor wore clothes
All ears tuned for the verdict
All eyes glued to the screen
We've come to accept as real
Anticipating denial
Of our heart-felt appeal

The Sound
for Robert Bly

Are you listening?
I am here.
Do you hear me burn?

Difficult
To hear me
In classes, or on buses.

But listen,
I am here
In a blind man's tears.

What is
That stealthy breathing?
The wind inside the dead.

The Moment

The ocean splashed
Over the rocks
While trees exploded
Along the dusty path

An instant of sunlight
Illuminated the cedars
As seagulls dipped
Above the wilderness of waves

At the edge of the beach
A fir tree tried to sleep
While greedy green weeds
Played a cool jazz beat

An old clown collapsed
Inside the silence of his mask

Old Woman's Dream #3

I found a penny on the ground, & picked it up. When I looked at it again, in my hand, I saw that it was really a small yellow flower. The color of the flower began to spread onto my hands, then my arms. Soon, I was yellow all over, & I burst out singing.

Crop Damage

In Nova Scotia
We risked our lives
Running with outlaws
Across the landscape
Beset by hailstones
Lips smacking
On thoughts of fresh tomatoes

The property damage:
The ducks, the cattle,
The wounded horses
Grass beaten down
Dance postponed
While desperate fields wept
Red with wounded tomatoes

Sonnet In D Minor

A kiss echoed
Shining & clear
Across the street
Classically villainous
Wounded animals hide
In the ecstatic jungle
They do not believe
In mirrors
Fur like onyx
Black vibrations
Against exuberant leaves
In cold sunlight
A spinning frenzy
A loud caress

Paradox Of Intersections

Every other busy intersection
Reveals a single dusty shoe
Or a flattened single glove

Their mates are gone
Though little movies come along
Flashing images of a conjured past

Later the shoes run away
& the gloves wave goodbye
Until the inevitable intersection passes

Littered with lost kisses & near misses

More Perspective

If you live on
A river or stream,
You must float
In place. You will need
A good anchor.

*

Vega glitters
In the northwest.
The stars above
The curved edge
Of the horizon
Match the stars
In front of you.

*

Bundle up & go outside.
The sky will look bigger
Than it does on paper.

Cape May Storm

Winds burn up the sea,
Lifting curtains from the surface
& slamming them
Across the wood shingled houses,
Growths on the arm of the cape.

Storm doors whip loose,
& patches of shingles
Are ripped off & thrown aloft.

They find slivers & pieces
Of their neighbor's roofs
When they hoe their gardens
In the inevitable spring.

Driving easterlies
Throw glassy spears,
Soaking gray, weathered shingles,
Until one side of each house
Is drenched to black.

The roof-ridges swell,
Then later
Shrink & settle, deformed.

When the soaked house
Dries in the sun,
Clouds of steam rise up,
& naive strangers alert the firehouse.

Sea Change

Clouds are laughing. Rain is ending. The old clown sits in revery. Later, a tornado rearranged his priorities. Now, he has a line of sight to the ocean, but his gaze is inward, toward humility.

The Run

for Harry Smith

We cannot hope
When the white flame is gone
That other fires don't burn
Under the flags of ancient ice
Beneath the tears of regret
Beyond the edge of light

Far from their overheated dens
Cold men run to the end
Down the darkened passing lanes
To strange gardens of fire
In wombs where they began
Beyond the porcelain moon

We'll feel no pain for what we've been
Even if it's never spring again

Animal Behavior

Some animals
Will only love you
If you are part
Of their pack.

Some animals
Will try to eat you
Even if you
Are their offspring.

Some animals
Will chew off
Their own feet
To escape a trap.

Some animals
Are always ready
To run away, listening
To live another day.

Some animals
Howl, while others
Growl, or snarl.
Some purr or smile.

Some animals
Don't even have
Any fur.
What kind of animal

Is that, over there?

For The Living Dead

For The Living Dead

1.
I rise with an effort
I feel the dead
They vibrate
In my foggy heart
Like icebergs colliding
In oceans of blood

I am alone
I sit by my window
I become a stone
Like stagnant water
Or steady drumming
I was once a prisoner too

I hear again
The familiar beat
Inside my heart
The divine rhythm
Of the countless dead
The rainstorms of light

2.
The zombies are revolting
They are crude in their culinary habits
Eating the flesh of the living
Raw with no seasoning
Duly elected representatives
With secret term limits

Sound the alarm
The flesh-eaters are in the house
They are slow but they keep on coming
They are mesmerized by fireworks
They like to run amok
When they aren't milling aimlessly

Zombies have no sex lives
They share the despair of the wolfman
Drunk on power under the full moon
Soaked in gasoline waiting for a light
Enflamed by love & hate
Counting down to the final insult

3.
A cipher falls dead in the snow
From a bus of discontinued androids
Last year's models obsolete versions
Of absolute ideals polished
To insane shines that reflect
The light that cannot be silenced

Jolly gunshots wound our pride
Armies of pleasure reap
Rewards of perfect cartoon murders
Buddhas smithereened by friendly fire
Floating in rivers of polite bodies
Joyfully waving their black flags

They are the human furniture
They are the living dishrags
They are the constant reminders
They are the ruined fortresses
Engorged on cloned flesh
Fitted with artificial hearts

4.
In the post-apocalyptic world
The zombies are loosely organized
With no zombie leader
They wander in random abandon
Trying to play various musical instruments
But their rhythm is shot

A small group of human survivors
Still comb their hair & wear make-up
Drooling & shuffling their feet
The zombies are mystified
By the smallest most subtle stimuli
But their haunted bony faces never smile

In the land of the dead
If a zombie bites you
You become a zombie too
You become a soldier in the zombie army
Sharing a goal with no sense of purpose
With an inner drive to obey

5.
The red bird still sings
In the green earth tree
In the airtight shopping mall
In the fenced-off arena
In shadows of tall buildings
In shacks of toothpicks

Robots built by zombies
Then put in charge
The doors are all locked
Impervious to your meat cleavers
Oblivious to your howls of pain
Ungrateful for your sacrifices

We navigate by dead reckoning
Our options are greatly reduced
We search in vain for a way out
Disguised by decadent cosmetics
The sentries at the gate are drunk
When the invasion comes they will die

6.
What can we do
What do we know
We who are barely human
We who have broken the 7th seal
We who have left the gate open
We who have stolen the Golden Fleece

Now the ghosts swallow us
We sullenly celebrate their loss
Our eyes opened wide as greed
Our diamonds soaked in blood
The coldest heads prevail
To organize the slaughter

Where have we been
What have we done
We mounted the final burial mound
We heard again the ancient last rites
We cloned sheep by the herd
We unleashed the living dead

7.
The robots are in formation
Speaking in unison
They all have the same face
Humorously humorless
They bow & scrape
Without relish or anguish

Robot malfunctions
Are inconvenient
Animated by artificial energy
Their movements are spooky
Unaware of planned obsolescence
Or constant surveillance

They make good household servants
They make good food service workers
They don't mind piece-work
Efficient & cost effective
Prison guards, they
Know no fear

8.
They don't need names
They don't have dreams
They don't throw temper tantrums
They're not ticklish
They don't itch much
They never need vacations

They don't get pregnant
They don't get drunk
They don't smoke
They don't eat or shit
They know not art
They hardly ever fart

A robot may be decommissioned
When a better model is developed
Many of the latest prototypes
Are biodegradable
They utilize virtual fibers
To simulate the naturally organic

9.
The severed head of Orpheus screams
Among the ashes of ancestors
Among the names carved into stone
In secret caves & hidden places
In tedious epics of doomed voyages
To the edge of the world

Organic life is prone to rot
Wooden puppets become brittle
Formaldehyde replaces blood
When the machine rules
Over the maker of machines
Which ones are the tools

Ghost lost before the body
Toy soldier left out in the rain
Hollow & impervious to pain
The pounding of robot feet
Grows louder by the parameter
Drowning out the earths heart

10.
I feel the spirits of the dead
They explode like seedpods
A thousand downy spheres
Doors that won't stay closed
Locks meant to be broken
Dandelions born in the wind

Beats of light drummed by spirits
Into the pulsating heart of sound
Into the unsanctified dirt
Out to the edges of space
Through the wounded waters
Beyond the toxic pain of time

I hear the call of light
Through the mechanical darkness
Through the marching shadows
Through the neutral rocks
The stale bread that feeds
The dreams of the anemic world

Eric Greinke is the author of several books of poetry, fiction & non-fiction. He has been active in the American small press since the late sixties. He has a Master's degree in Social Work from Grand Valley State University & twenty-five years experience working with disturbed & disabled children. He has also taught creative writing in an alternative high school & worked in the Michigan Poets In The Schools program. He enjoys hiking, fishing, kayaking & playing blues guitar. He lives in a century old cottage on a Northern lake.

Louis E. Bourgeois
Alice, $6.00
Kirby Congdon
God Is Dead (again), $20.00
Selected Poems & Prose Poems, $15.00
Hugh Fox
Time & Other Poems, $6.00
Blood Cocoon - Selected Poems of Connie Fox, $15.00
Eric Greinke
Selected Poems 1972-2005, $20.00
The Drunken Boat & Other Poems From
The French Of Arthur Rimbaud, $15.95
Kerry Shawn Keys
The Burning Mirror, $14.95
Richard Kostelanetz
PO/EMS, $6.00
Ronnie M. Lane
Morpheus Rising, $6.00
Linda Lerner
Living In Dangerous Times, $6.00
Lyn Lifshin
In Mirrors, $15.00
Glenna Luschei
Seedpods, $6.00
Total Immersion, $15.00
Stanley Nelson
Pre-Socratic Points & Other New Poems, $15.00
Limbos For Amplified Harpsichord, $17.95
Roseanne Ritzema, (Editor)
Inside The Outside - An Anthology of
Avant-Garde American Poets, $29.95
Lynne Savitt
The Deployment Of Love In Pineapple Twilight, $6.00
Harry Smith & Eric Greinke
Up North, $6.00
Ben Tibbs
Poems, $6.00
Lloyd Van Brunt
Delirium, $6.00
Leslie H. Whitten Jr.
The Rebel - Poems by Charles Baudelaire, $7.50
A.D. Winans
This Land Is Not My Land, $6.00.
The Other Side of Broadway - Selected Poems, $18.00